# Braşov

*Braşov Old Town seen from Braşov Fortress*

## Feel the Pulse of

## Transylvania in 3 Days

By Olivia-Petra Coman

## ⊕ UNANCHOR

# Table of Contents

# Day 1
=============

## 9:00 am -- Breakfast/Coffee & sweets at 'Come Back'

- **Price:** RON 15.00 (for a single adult)
- **Duration:** 30 minutes
- **Address:** Piaţa Sfatului nr. 7
  Telephone: +40770352866
  Opening hours:
  7:30am-10:00pm (Mon-Sun)
  Credit cards accepted.

Grab a bite and sample the delicious décor of this cozy German bakery.

**Recommendations:** Try the emmentaler bun with a delicious cappuccino (served with ice cream on hot summer days).

## 9:30 am -- 'Come Back' to Council Square

- **Duration:** 5 minutes

Surprise, you are already in Council Square!

# 9:35 am -- Council Square

- **Price:** FREE
- **Duration:** 10 minutes
- **Address:** Piaţa Sfatului

Walk around Council Square, take pictures, and feed the pigeons.

**Trivia:** The Council Square has been the place for annual markets since 1364, welcoming local and international merchants. Witches were also punished here. The building in the center of the square is the Council House, erected in 1420 and initially serving as a watch tower. Later on, it started to function as the town hall until 1876. It currently hosts the local History Museum. The lights of the town's Christmas tree are annually lit in Council Square on St. Nicholas Day (December 6th). It is unofficially declared as the most beautiful Christmas tree in Romania, year after year.

## 9:45 am -- Council Square to the First Romanian School

- **Duration:** 15 minutes

Explore the old streets of Braşov and stop for a few minutes to look at the town's oldest high school, 'Andrei Şaguna', built in 1850 and cultural home to many Romanian elites (students and teachers of this institution) - composers Ciprian Porumbescu and Gheorghe Dima, poet Octavian Goga, linguists Sextil Puşcariu and Titu Maiorescu, historian Vasile Goldiş - to name but a few.

**Directions:** Go straight ahead on Gheorghe Bariţiu Street for one block and continue on Constantin Brâncoveanu Street. You will see 'Andrei Şaguna' National College on your left in 100 meters. Stop for pictures and continue on Constantin Brâncoveanu Street until you reach a large square. You are now in Union Square [Piaţa Unirii] and the First Romanian School is situated diagonally from where you now stand. Cross the square, enter the courtyard, and follow the path. The museum is on your left and St. Nicholas Church is on your right.

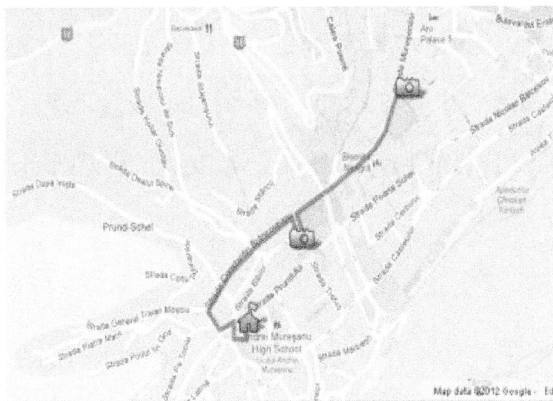

# 10:00 am -- The First Romanian School

- **Price:** RON 5.00 (for a single adult)
- **Duration:** 1 hour
- **Address:** Piaţa Unirii nr. 2-3
  Telephone: +40268511411
  Opening hours:
  9am-5pm (Mon-Sun)
  Cash only.

The First Romanian School gives you the perfect occasion to understand the sources of Romanian/Transylvanian culture and civilization.

**Trivia:** Attested from 1495 but dating back to at least 1390, the building still displays a typical Transylvanian classroom, a 16th century printing press, and some very old books, including 'Omiliarul', a school manual considered to have been written in the 11th-12th century.

**Tip:** Take a few minutes to visit Sf. Nicolae [St. Nicholas] Church, dating back to 1292.

**Additional info:** Admission fee for students: 3 lei

**Facilities:** Guide (in German, French, Russian), Gift shop, Toilets

## 11:00 am -- The First Romanian School to Rope Street

- **Duration:** 30 minutes

You are only half an hour away from one of the town's curiosities.

Don't forget to stop for a few minutes at Schei Gate, built between 1827 and 1828 by the people in Schei District to enable their access into Brașov, in a period of heightened traffic.

**Directions:** Exit the yard and turn right. Exit Union Square and turn right again on Prundului Street. Go straight ahead until you reach a circus. Schei Gate is before you, so it may be time for some pictures. Continue straight ahead for 100 more meters and you will find Rope Street on your right.

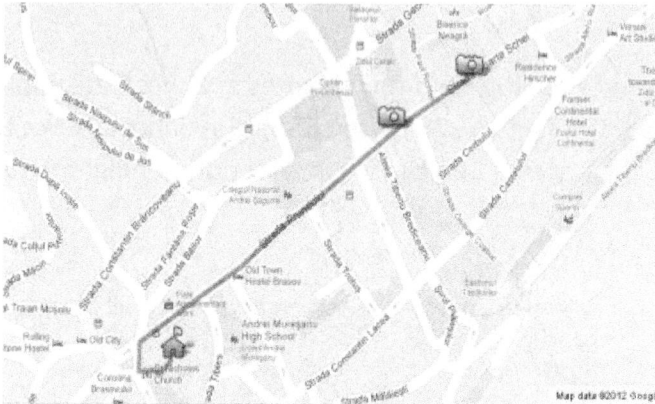

# 11:30 am  -- Rope Street

- **Price:** FREE
- **Duration:** 10 minutes
- **Address:** Strada Sforii

Observe and take pictures.

**Trivia:** Rope Street is the narrowest street in Braşov and in Southeastern Europe. Initially built as a corridor for firemen's use, it is 80 meters long, with a width varying between 111 and 135 centimeters.

## 11:40 am -- Rope Street to Cable Car

- **Duration:** 15 minutes

Within minutes, you will enjoy one of the best vistas over Braşov.

**Directions:** At the end of Rope Street, turn left and go straight ahead until you reach a circus. Continue straight ahead for two blocks. Turn right and go up Suişul Castelului Street. Go up the steps and continue on the alley until you reach the cable car.

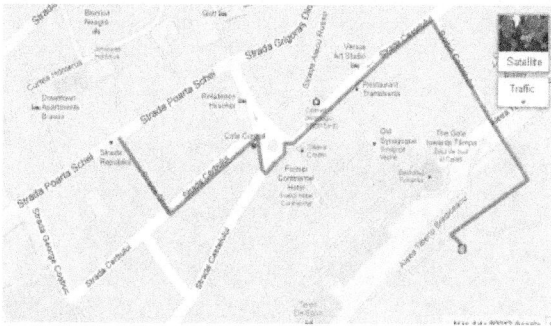

# 11:55 am  -- Mount Tâmpa (964 m)

- **Price:** RON 16.00 (for a single adult)
- **Duration:** 1 hour and 20 minutes
- **Address:** Tâmpa
  Opening hours:
  12pm-6pm (Mon); 9:30am-6pm (Tue-Fri); 9:30am-7pm (Sat-Sun)
  Last ride (up): 5:45pm (Mon-Fri); 6:45pm (Sat-Sun)
  Last ride (down): 6pm (Mon-Fri); 7pm (Sat-Sun)

Take the cable car up and enjoy the fresh mountain air as you take pictures of the only natural reserve in the world located in the center of a town.

*Local's Tip:* *Walk to the bellevue and try to recognize the landmarks of Braşov seen from above.*

**Additional info:**

If you feel like trekking, buy a one-way pass (10 lei).

Children under 12 will pay 6 lei for a one-way pass and 9 lei for a return pass.

# 1:15 pm -- Cable Car to the Black Church

- **Duration:** 20 minutes

Steps away from discovering one of the landmarks of Braşov.

**Directions:** Go straight ahead and turn left at the end of the alley. Go down the steps and continue on Dobrogeanu Gherea Street. Turn left at the end of the street. Walk straight ahead on Nicolae Bălcescu Street and bear right after two blocks. Turn right at the end of the street and walk straight ahead. You are now in Council Square. Turn left. You should see the Black Church. The entrance into the church is opposite to where you now stand.

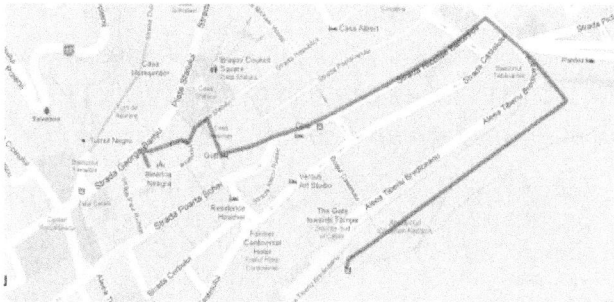

# 1:35 pm -- The Black Church

- **Price:** RON 8.00 (for a single adult)
- **Duration:** 20 minutes
- **Address:** Curtea Johannes Honterus 2
  Telephone: +40268511824
  Opening hours:
  May - Oct: 10am-7pm (Tue-Sat); 12pm-7pm (Sun);
  Nov - Apr: 10am-3pm (Tue-Sat); 12pm-3pm (Sun);
  Closed Mon

Go into the Black Church and take pictures. If allowed, climb into the tower to see the largest mobile bell in the country, weighing 6 tons.

**Trivia:** Following the fire set by the invading Habsburg forces on April 21st 1689, part of the structure of this immense Gothic construction was destroyed and the church was later on referred to as the '*Black Church*'.

*Local's Tip: There are organ concerts held here on Tuesdays (June, September; 6pm-6:30pm) and on Tuesdays, Thursdays, and Saturdays (July, August; 6pm-6:30pm). Tickets: 8 lei*

**Additional info:** Admission fee for: students: 5 lei; children: 3 lei

**Facilities:** Cash only; Gift shop

**Variants:** If visiting on Mondays, when the Black Church is closed, head directly to Mureşenilor Street and check out the bookshops selling beautiful postcards and books on different regions of Romania in various languages (they are good value and make terrific souvenirs and gifts; the information and amazing photographs they provide will definitely convince you).

## 1:55 pm -- The Black Church to După Ziduri Street

- **Duration:** 5 minutes

Get better acquainted with Braşov by walking behind its town walls.

**Directions:** Walk straight ahead until you reach a pedestrian crossing. Cross the street and go around the big building on your right. You will see a brook on your left. You are on După Ziduri Street. You will immediately see Graft Bastion on your right and the steps to the White Tower on your left.

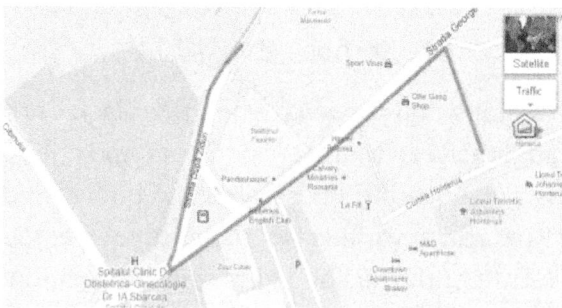

# 2:00 pm -- Graft Bastion

- **Price:** RON 7.00 (for a single adult)
- **Duration:** 35 minutes
- **Address:** Strada După Ziduri
  Telephone: +40268474662
  Opening hours:
  10am-6pm (Tue-Sun); Mon: closed
  Cash only.

Go up the stairs and imagine how the old medieval times must have felt like.

**Trivia:** The bastion dates back to the 15th century and was built to connect the White Tower with the town fortifications.

*Local's Tip: Climb the steps to the White Tower. The view over the town center is fantastic. Opening hours: 10am-6pm (Tue-Sun); Mon: closed. Admission fees: 7 lei (adults); 4 lei (students, retired)*

**Additional info**: Admission fee for: students, retired: 4 lei

**Facilities:** Gift shop

**Variants:** If visiting on Mondays, when the two attactions are closed, head to lunch earlier.

# 2:35 pm -- După Ziduri Street to 'Festival '39'

- **Duration:** 15 minutes

Head to the town's hippest street to have late lunch.

**Directions:** Turn right at the end of După Ziduri Street and walk straight ahead. Turn right into Mureşenilor Street and walk straight ahead until you reach the traffic lights. Cross the street and go straight ahead on Sf. Ioan Street. At the end of the street, turn left. You are now on Republicii Street. Go straight ahead; 'Festival '39' is on your right, 150 meters ahead.

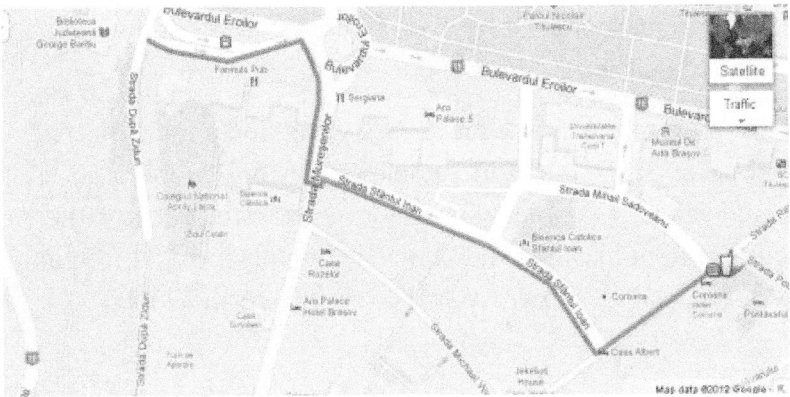

# 2:50 pm -- Late lunch at 'Festival '39'

- **Price:** RON 40.00 (for a single adult)
- **Duration:** 1 hour and 30 minutes
- **Address:** Strada Republicii nr. 62
  Telephone: +40743339909
  Opening hours:
  7am - 12am (Mon-Sun)
  Credit cards accepted.

Have lunch in one of the most popular restaurants in Braşov, 'Festival '39'.

**Recommendations:** Don't even think not to order desserts! They are delicious!

**Tips:** If visiting on very hot days, try and find a table on the terrace and take in the incredible energy of Republicii Street. If you finish lunch earlier, walk into the shops found on either sides of Republicii Street. They may be pricier than those in other areas of the town, but they're still worth a look.

# 4:20 pm -- 'Festival '39' to Braşov Fortress

- **Duration:** 40 minutes

Embark on a scenic walk to Braşov Fortress.

**Directions:** Turn right, walk to the end of the street and cross the street. Walk across the park and cross Nicolae Iorga Street. You will see a café (Galleria) in front of you and the Art High School (Liceul de Artă) next to it. Take the street passing before the high school (Colonel Buzoianu Street) and turn left after one block (Maior Ion Cranţa Street). Follow this street until you reach the fortress.

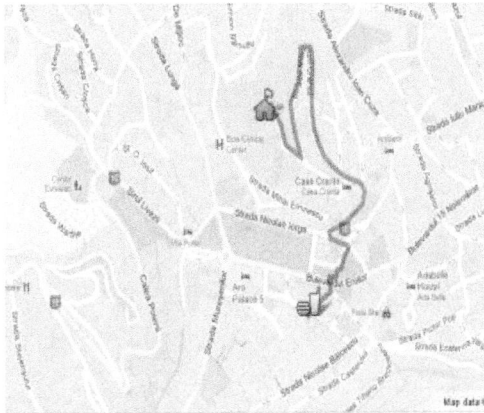

# 5:00 pm -- Braşov Fortress

- **Price:** FREE
- **Duration:** 25 minutes
- **Address:** Dealul Cetăţii

Take your time, walk around the fortress, and enjoy the view.

**Trivia:** Attested from 1580, the fortress was destroyed because of battles or of fires over its history. It even served as a prison for Turkish and French prisoners and as a health care facility for plague patients in the 18th century.

*Local's Tip: You may find the gates locked, as the restaurant that used to operate inside was closed. Walk by the fortress walls instead.*

## 5:25 pm -- Braşov Fortress to Paradisul Acvatic

- **Price:** RON 12.00 (for a single adult)
- **Duration:** 20 minutes

Get a taxi by phone (see Appendix), use the *Clever Taxi* app, or order an Uber.

# 5:45 pm -- Paradisul Acvatic

- **Price:** RON 30.00 (for a single adult)
- **Duration:** 2 hours
- **Address:** Bulevardul Griviţei nr. 2F-2G
  Telephone: +40268440070
  Opening hours:
  2pm-10pm (Mon); 11am-10pm (Tue-Fri); 10am-10pm (Sat-Sun)
  Credit cards accepted.

Two hours to relax after the long walks of the day! Several pools and saunas, hot tubs, massage, solarium - you name it, **Paradisul Acvatic** has it.

*Local's Tip: Enjoy the cool evening air by swimming in the outside pool in summer close to closing time and feel the snowflakes on your skin in the outside hot pool in winter.*

## 7:45 pm -- Paradisul Acvatic to 'Trattoria del Chianti'

- **Price:** RON 14.00 (for a single adult)
- **Duration:** 25 minutes

It's time to get back into town!

Get a taxi by phone (see Appendix), use the *Clever Taxi* app, or order an Uber.

# 8:10 pm -- Dinner at 'Trattoria del Chianti'

- **Price:** RON 50.00 (for a single adult)
- **Duration:** 2 hours and 50 minutes
- **Address:** Strada Brânduşelor nr. 100
  Telephone: +40268546087
  Opening hours: 12pm-11pm (Mon-Sun)
  Credit cards accepted.

'Trattoria del Chianti' is one of the best Italian restaurants in Braşov.

**Recommendations:** Salads, seafood, desserts (especially the apple strudel with ice cream, the apple cake, and the profiterole).

*Local's Tip:* *Enjoy the cool mountain breeze on summer nights by asking for a table on the terrace or in the garden.*

# Day 2

=============

## 9:00 am -- Pretzels at 'Covrigăria Gigi'

- **Price:** RON 4.00 (for a single adult)
- **Duration:** 10 minutes
- **Address:** Strada Nicolae Bălcescu/Piaţa Teatrului

Have 2 or 3 pretzels to start the day.

**Recommendations:** Try poppy or sesame pretzels and the exquisite pretzels filled with sour cherry jam.

**Variants:** At weekends, start your day at 10:15am, skip brunch, and head from the Pedestrian Street directly to Muncii Bus Stop and continue with the rest of the suggested program. Parc Aventura may be crowded, so you might want to get there earlier and avoid queuing for the safety equipment.

## 9:10 am -- 'Covrigăria Gigi' to Dobrogeanu Gherea Street

- **Duration:** 5 minutes

Start of your morning walk over one of the town's hills.

**Directions:** Go straight ahead on Nicolae Bălcescu Street until you reach 'Star' Department Store. The following street (the one that goes up the hill) is Dobrogeanu Gherea.

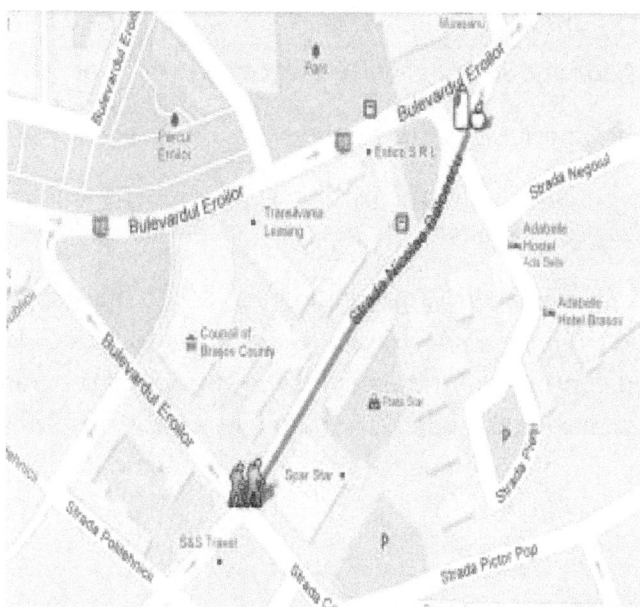

# 9:15 am -- Dealul Melcilor

- **Price:** FREE
- **Duration:** 30 minutes
- **Address:** Dobrogeanu Gherea Street

Scenic walk over Dealul Melcilor [Snails Hill].

*Local's Tip: When you reach the top of the hill, take the first street on the left before Cincinat Pavelescu Street and climb all the way to the water tower. The view is fantastic!*

## 9:45 am -- Dobrogeanu Gherea Street to Pedestrian Street

*   **Duration:** 15 minutes

**Directions:** Continue straight ahead on Tâmpei Street and turn right on Valea Cetăţii Blvd. Go straight ahead until you reach the park. Enter the park and go down the Pedestrian Street.

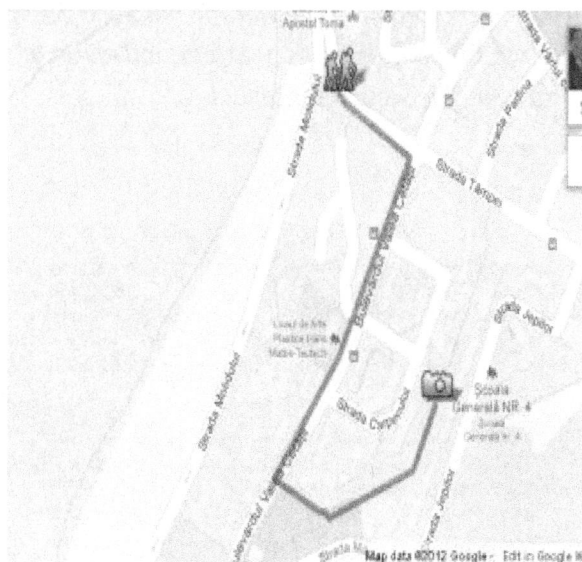

# 10:00 am -- Pedestrian Street (Pietonala)

- **Duration:** 15 minutes
- **Address:** Pietonală Răcădău

Enjoy the tranquillity of the pedestrian street.

## 10:15 am -- Pedestrian Street to 'Bricks'

- **Duration:** 5 minutes

Head to 'Bricks' for brunch.

**Directions:** Go straight ahead and cross the street when you reach the end of the pedestrian street. 'Bricks' is now in front of you.

# 10:20 am -- Brunch at 'Bricks'

- **Price:** RON 30.00 (for a single adult)
- **Duration:** 1 hour and 10 minutes
- **Address:** Strada Eftimie Murgu nr. 1
  Telephone: +40268324148
  Opening hours:
  10am-12am (Mon-Fri);
  12pm-12am (Sat);
  3pm-12am (Sun)
  Cash only.

Very good and cozy Italian restaurant, also serving Romanian traditional dishes.

**Recommendations:** The pizzas, the cheese sauce, the tiramisu.

**Tips:** Have brunch on the terrace on hot summer days, order fresh lemonade, and relax.

## 11:30 am -- 'Bricks' to Muncii Bus Stop (Livada Poştei)

- **Duration:** 10 minutes

Head to Muncii Bus Stop.

**Directions:** Turn right and go straight ahead until you reach the end of the street, then turn right. The bus stop is 100 meters ahead.

## 11:40 am -- Muncii Bus Stop (Livada Poştei) to Judeţean Bus Stop (Livada Poştei)

- **Price:** RON 2.00 (for a single adult)
- **Duration:** 15 minutes

Take Bus no. 31 or 32 or Trolleybus no. 3 or 10 to Judeţean Bus Stop, Direction Livada Poştei.

## 11:55 am -- Judeţean Bus Stop (Livada Poştei) to Judeţean Bus Stop (Noua)

- **Duration:** 5 minutes

Cross the street to the opposite bus stop.

**Directions:** Go straight ahead, pass the circus, and arrive at a pedestrian crossing. The bus stop is on the other side of the crossing.

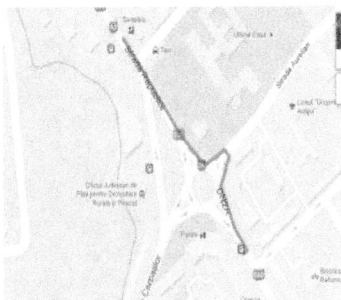

## 12:00 pm -- Judeţean Bus Stop (Noua) to Ştrand Noua Bus Stop (Noua)

- **Price:** RON 2.00 (for a single adult)
- **Duration:** 20 minutes

Take Bus no. 17 or 35 to Ştrand Noua Bus Stop, Direction Noua.

## 12:20 pm -- Ştrand Noua Bus Stop (Noua) to Parc Aventura

- **Duration:** 5 minutes

Only 5 minutes away from an adrenaline rush!

**Directions:** Go straight ahead and turn left after one block. Go straight ahead for one block. The entrance to Parc Aventura is on your right, 100 meters ahead.

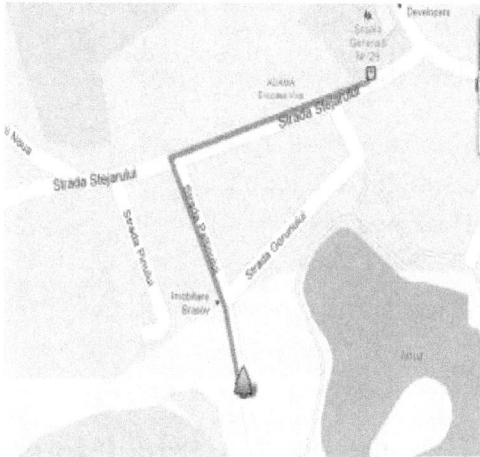

# 12:25 pm -- Parc Aventura

- **Price:** RON 40.00 (for a single adult)
- **Duration:** 3 hours
- **Address:** Strada Paltinului 16bis
  Telephone: +40268337817
  Opening hours: 10am-5pm (Mon-Sun)
  Cash only.

- **Website:** http://www.parc-aventura.ro/

Force your limits in the largest adventure park in Eastern Europe!

**Recommendations:** You will be required to start with an easier track (Yellow or Green), continue with a more difficult one (Blue or Red), and the last one you attempt to complete should be the Black one.

*Local's Tip: If you're fit, start with the most difficult of the easy tracks, Green 3, and continue with Red 1 or 2 if you want to give the Black track a go. If it's your first time in an adventure park, start with Yellow 1, 2, or 3, continue with Blue 1 or 2, and then finish the day with Red 1. And you can always have a lemonade and some sweets on the terrace inside the park.*

**Warning!** Please call or send an e-mail before going if it's in winter. During this period, Parc Aventura might be open only at weekends, on public holidays, and on school holidays.

**Variants:** For those who are not keen on giving this park a go, head for the nearby **Braşov Zoo** instead (see Appendix/Wildlife) or do a trek (see Appendix/Trekking).

## 3:25 pm -- Parc Aventura to Ştrand Noua Bus Stop (Livada Poştei) [via Noua Lake]

- **Duration:** 20 minutes

It's time to get back into town and relax for the rest of the evening.

**Directions:** You can already see the lake. Turn right when you exit Parc Aventura and follow the path around the lake. Continue to follow the path around the lake until you see a parking lot. Go straight ahead until you reach Stejarului Street. Turn right and go straight ahead for one block. Turn right again. The bus stop is 100 meters ahead.

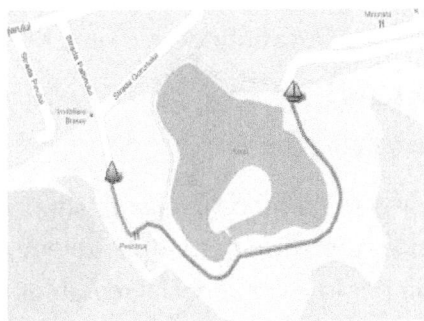

## 3:45 pm -- Ştrand Noua Bus Stop (back into town) to accommodation

- **Price:** RON 2.00 (for a single adult)
- **Duration:** 30 minutes

Take Bus no. 17 or 35, go back into town, and head to your accommodation.

Take some time to relax or simply take a well-deserved shower after the struggles in the adventure park, change and go out for dinner in a very special restaurant located in the heart of the town.

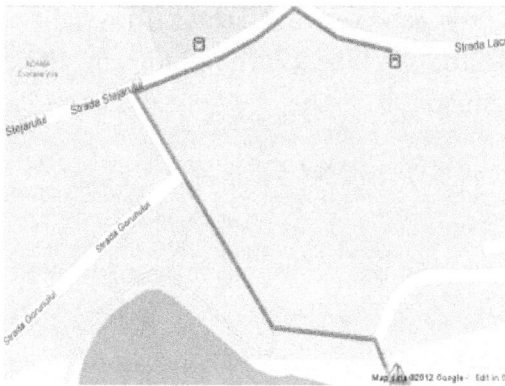

# 7:00 pm -- The Hockey Pub

- **Price:** RON 45.00 (for a single adult)
- **Duration:** 2 hours
- **Address:** Str. Nicolae Bălcescu nr. 12
  Telephone: +40731919919
  Opening hours:
  1pm-12:30am (Mon-Thu & Sun); 1pm-1am (Fri-Sat)
  Credit cards accepted.

My favourite place to eat in Braşov. I think there's nothing else to be added. If closed, head to **Bistro de l'Arte** instead.

Still--

**Recommendations:** All the soups, the caramel brownie, the cheesecake, the gomboţi, the best burgers in town.

**Tips:** Book by calling, especially on Tuesdays (pub quiz) and at weekends. This restaurant is always packed. Vegetarians will have plenty of choices. And if I mentioned the quiz, it is in English, the fee is 1 leu per person and tons of fun around nice people are guaranteed for at least 3hrs and a half.

# Day 3

==============

## 6:10 am -- Train to Saschiz

- **Price:** RON 15.50 (for a single adult)
- **Duration:** 2 hours and 45 minutes

Start your trip into the heart of Transylvania!

**Tips:**

- Don't forget to take two or three sandwiches and a few snacks with you, and at least one bottle of water.
- Have cash on you (around 150-200 lei), as it may be difficult to find ATMs or to pay by credit card.
- Travel light, as you will be required to climb and walk a lot.

## Variants:

### A) Saschiz & Viscri

Get there: Due to the remoteness of Viscri (UNESCO World Heritage Site), this daytrip can only be completed by taxi (Price: 200 lei; call +40744603884 (Adrian Gurzun)) or by a rental car. There isn't public transport to Viscri either from Rupea or from Buneşti.

Do: After visiting Saschiz Fortified Church, continue to Viscri. You will discover un unspoilt traditional village, with colorful handmade souvenirs like the famous Viscri socks.

See: Viscri Fortified Church, dated 1210, the oldest fortified church in Transylvania.

Opening times: March-October: 10am-1pm & 3pm-6pm (Mon-Sun);
Key: In winter, ask for it in house no. 141, at castle guard Sara Dootz;
Telephone: +40742077506;
Ticket: 8 lei (adults); 4 lei (students, groups);
Facilities: Guide (for more than 5 people, included in the ticket price), Gift shop, Café, Parking, Toilets, Cash Only

## B) Saschiz & Rupea

Get there: Take any bus from Saschiz heading to Braşov or Bucharest between 7:21am and 9:21pm (departure: Tg. Mureş) or between 9:15am and 9:50pm (departure: Bistriţa), every 2 hours; Time: 45'; Ticket: 6 lei

Do: After visiting Saschiz Fortified Church, continue to Rupea. Climb the hill to **Rupea Fortress**. The view is beautiful and the fortress is in my opinion the most dramatic in Romania.

See: Rupea Fortress was probably built in the 10th century, although recent archaeological diggings in the area have proved that the history of the region links to the Dacian times (more than 2000 years ago). Rupea Fortress has been open since June 15th 2013; Opening hours: 9am-8pm (Mo-Sun); Admission fee: 10 lei (adults); 5 lei (children); 8 lei (organized groups)

Return to Braşov: Take any bus from Rupea heading to Braşov or Bucharest 7:21am and 9:21pm (departure: Tg. Mureş) or between 10am and 10:30pm (departure: Bistriţa), every 2 hours; Time: 1h16'; Ticket: 20 lei | 18 lei

# 8:55 am -- Saschiz Railway Station to Saschiz Fortress

* 
* **Duration:** 1 hour and 35 minutes

Head into the center of Saschiz, where the high tower is found.

If you need additional directions, the Tourist Information Office is next to the fortified church.

Opening hours: 10am-6pm

**Directions:** Take the road along the church for one block; you are about to start your climb. Follow the signs to 'CETATE' (Fortress).

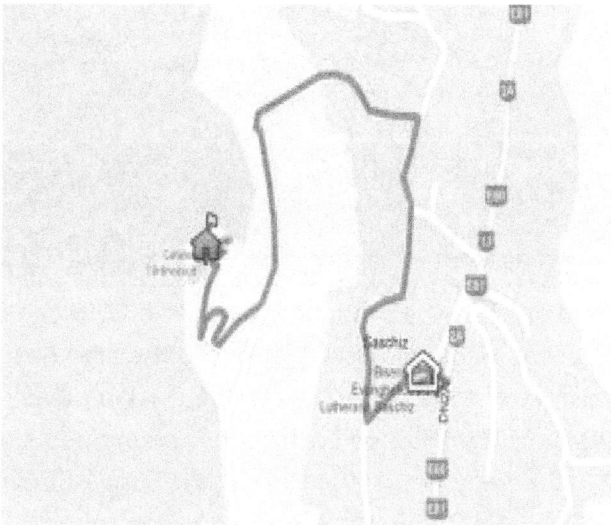

# 10:30 am -- Saschiz Fortress

- **Price:** FREE
- **Duration:** 1 hour
- **Address:** 2 km from Saschiz Village

You are rewarded with a beautiful view over Saschiz, so be sure to walk around the walls and take many pictures.

**Trivia:** The fortress was built to protect the inhabitants of Saschiz and of the surrounding villages from invasions. The only structure that is still intact is the 65 m deep well that it is said to connect - via an underground tunnel - the fortress and the center of Saschiz.

**Tip:** One of the outer walls opposite that facing the village (Northwestern) has the year 1347 inscribed on it. This is the year when the construction of the fortress began.

## 11:30 am -- Saschiz Fortress to Saschiz Fortified Church

- **Duration:** 1 hour and 30 minutes

Head back into the village and don't forget to buy some world-famous Saschiz jams [including the delicate milk jam], sold at the Tourist Information Office. If you are hungry, stop for lunch at **Hanul Cetății.**

**Directions:** Take the same road back into the center of the village.

# 1:00 pm -- Saschiz Fortified Church

- **Price:** RON 6.00 (for a single adult)
- **Duration:** 1 hour
- **Address:** Saschiz Village
  UNESCO World Heritage Site
  Telephone: +40744179039
  Opening hours: 10am-6pm (Mon & Wed-Sun); Tue: closed
  Cash only.

Discover the **Evangelical Church of Saschiz**.

**Trivia:** It was built at the end of the 15th century by the Saxon colonists and it is impressive by the way in which the fortifying structures were adapted to the elements of the church.

**Additional information:** Admission fee: 3 lei (children)

**Facilities:** Guide (in Romanian and German), Parking

## 2:00 pm -- Saschiz to Sighişoara

- **Price:** RON 2.00 (for a single adult)
- **Duration:** 45 minutes

From the center of Saschiz, take any bus heading to Tg. Mureş between 10:59am and 10:59pm (departure: Bucharest) or to Bistriţa between 7:10am and 5:50pm (departure: Braşov), every 2 hours; Time: 6'

Ticket for buses headed to Tg. Mureş: 5 lei

# 2:45 pm -- Sighişoara Bus Station to Sighişoara Citadel

- **Duration:** 15 minutes

**Directions:** If you arrive at CAMBUS SA Bus Station (Strada Libertăţii nr. 53), go straight ahead on Libertăţii Street. In 3 blocks, you will reach Matei Basarab Blvd. Turn left and walk straight ahead for 2 blocks. Turn right on Anton Pann Street. Walk straight ahead; the entrance into the Citadel is within 2 blocks.

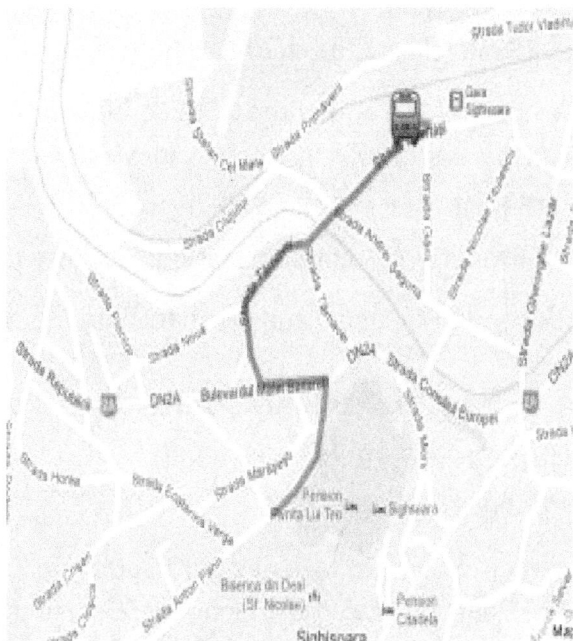

# 3:00 pm -- Sighişoara Citadel

- **Price:** FREE
- **Duration:** 2 hours and 45 minutes
- **Address:** Sighişoara
  UNESCO World Heritage Site
  Telephone: +40265771108

**Sighişoara** is one of the best preserved medieval citadels in Europe and the only one that's still inhabited!

**Trivia:** It dates back to the 12th century and was built by the Saxons invited by the King of Hungary to settle here and to defend the borders.

**Tips:** Lose yourself in the romantic atmosphere and explore the narrow streets. Have early dinner at one of the cozy cafés and bistros (around 5 o'clock; suggestions: **Casa Cositorarului, Casa cu Cerb**), but don't forget to climb into the Clock Tower and take in the view.

Opening times: 9am-4pm (Tue-Sun); Mon: closed

Ticket: 6 lei
Facilities: Guide (in Romanian, English, German), Gift shop, Parking (15 lei, only passenger cars)

**Local's Tip:** *If you have some time left, climb the Covered Staircase (Scara Şcolarilor) to the Church on the Hill (Biserica din Deal). It's a very romantic 'adventure'.*

## 5:45 pm -- Sighişoara Citadel to Sighişoara Railway Station

- **Duration:** 20 minutes

**Directions:** Exit the Citadel and turn right into Anton Pann Street. Walk straight ahead for two blocks, then turn right into Morii Street. Go straight ahead for a block and then turn left into Târnavei Street. Turn right at the end of the street. You are now on Libertăţii Street. The bus station (CAMBUS SA) and the railway station are two blocks ahead.

## 6:05 pm -- Sighişoara to Braşov

- **Price:** RON 39.70 (for a single adult)
- **Duration:** 2 hours and 30 minutes

Additionally, you can take any bus heading to Braşov or Bucharest between 8:38am and 10:38pm (departure: Tg. Mureş) or between 11:16am and 11:46pm (departure: Bistriţa), every 2 hours; Time: 2h8'; Ticket: 25 lei | 23 lei

In the remaining time, get to your accommodation, take a shower and relax. If you are not too tired, a Braşov stopover would not be complete without a party, so go out and have some fun!

# 10:00 pm -- Party at 'Il Caminetto'

- **Price:** RON 80.00 (for a single adult)
- **Duration:** 1 hour and 50 minutes
- **Address:** Piaţa Sfatului nr. 27
  Telephone: +400733940049
  Opening hours:
  10am-5am (Fri-Sat); Credit cards accepted.

Good and diverse music; fancy atmosphere [dress the part!].

'Good music isn't at the radio' is their motto. See for yourselves and keep an eye on their Facebook page - you might find an interesting event!

**Directions:** In the very center of Braşov. As simple as that.

**Tips:** Book your table-- rezervari@il-caminetto.ro. And if it happens to be a different day of the week from Friday and Saturday, see 'Appendix' for more info on ways to spend your night.

# Other daytrips

## A) Hărman & Sf. Gheorghe

### Get to Hărman:

*By bus:* for schedules and rates, see http://www.autogari.ro
*By train:* for schedules and rates, see http://www.infofer.ro/en/
*By car:* Take E574 (to Sf. Gheorghe) and turn left at the first crossroads after entering Hărman. Distance: 11 km; Time: 15'

### See in Hărman:

## Hărman Fortified Church

Why go there: Impressive fortified church dating back to the 13th century.
Opening hours: Summer (May-October): 9am-6pm (Mon-Sat); 10am-6am (Sun) & Winter (November-April): 10am-4pm (Mon-Sun) [Ring the bell if there is nobody there.]
Address: Strada Pieţii nr. 2
Telephone: +40748067962
Admission fee: 10 lei (adults); 5 lei (students)
Credit card accepted? No
Other facilities: Gift shop, Toilet, Parking

**Get from Hărman to Sf. Gheorghe:**

*By bus:* for schedules and rates, see http://www.autogari.ro
[Catch the bus by getting into the main road.]
*By train:* for schedules and rates, see http://www.infofer.ro/en/
*By car:* Go back to E574 and continue straight ahead to Sf.
Gheorghe; at the first crossroads, turn left. Distance: 27 km;
Time: 32'

## Do in Sf. Gheorghe:

Walk around the center and in the park.
Head to one of the best cake/ice cream parlors you'll ever try!

### Aria

Opening hours: 9am-7pm (Mon-Sat); 11am-7pm (Sun)
Address: Strada 1 Decembrie 1918 nr. 41
Telephone: +40267311808
Price range: $ (5-10)
Credit card accepted? Yes
Recommendations: Have a bowl of the delicious ice creams made from fresh fruit. Add whipped cream, chocolate sauce, fresh fruit, and Somlói galuska. Buy some exquisite cakes for later.

### Get back to Braşov from Sf. Gheorghe:

*By bus:* for schedules and rates, see http://www.autogari.ro
*By train:* for schedules and rates, see http://www.infofer.ro/en/
*By car:* Take E574 (to Braşov) and turn right at the first crossroads. Distance: 34 km; Time: 37'

# B) Buşteni & Sinaia

Get to Buşteni:

*By bus:* for schedules and rates, see http://www.autogari.ro

*By train:* for schedules and rates, see http://www.infofer.ro/en/

*By car:* Take E60 (to Bucharest). Distance: 36 km; Time: 34'

**See in Buşteni:**

If you have time, take the cable car to Sfinxul and Babele rock formations.

## Cantacuzino Castle

Why go there: Beautiful early 20thcentury castle and a stunning vista.

Opening hours: 10am-6pm (Mon-Thu) & 10am-7pm (Fri-Sun)

Address: Strada Zamora nr. 1

Telephone: +40244320520

Admission fee: Basic Tour - 20 lei (adults); 15 lei (students, retired); 10 lei (children aged 12-18); 7 lei (children aged 6-12); no charge (children under 6)

Credit card accepted? Yes

Other facilities: Guide (only in Romanian), Restaurant [try out Canta Cuisine, it is delicious!!], Café, Toilets, Gift shop, Parking

## Get from Buşteni to Sinaia:

*By bus:* for schedules and rates, see http://www.autogari.ro
*By train:* for schedules and rates, see http://www.infofer.ro/en/
*By car:* Continue on E60 (direction Bucharest) to Sinaia.
Distance: 11 km; Time: 17'

**See in Sinaia:**

# Peleş Castle [and Pelişor Castle]

Why go there: One of the most beautiful European castles!
Opening hours:
Mid-May – Mid-September:
Peleş: 11am-4:15pm (Wed); 9:15am-4:15pm (Thu-Sun); Mon,
Tue: closed
Pelişor: 11:15am-5:15pm; 10:15am-5:15pm (Thu-Sun); Mon,
Tue: closed
Mid-September – Mid-May:
Peleş & Pelişor: 11:15am-4:15pm (Wed); 9:15am-4:15pm (Thu-Sun); Mon, Tue: closed
Address: Strada Peleşului nr. 2
Telephone: +40244310918
Admission fee:
Peleş: Basic Tour – 20 lei (adults); 10 lei (retired); 5 lei (students, children, Euro<26 card)
Pelişor: 20 lei (adults); 10 lei (retired); 5 lei (students, children, Euro<26 card)
Credit card accepted? No
Other facilities: Guide (in Romanian, English, French, Italian, and Spanish), Toilets, Gift shop

# George Enescu Memorial House

Why go there: Cozy and colorful home of one of the greatest Romanian composers.

Opening hours: 10am-5pm (Tue-Sun); Mon: closed

Address: Strada Yehudi Menuhin nr. 2, Cumpătu District

Telephone: +40244311753

Admission fee: 6 lei (adults); 3 lei (retired); 1.50 lei (students)

Credit card accepted? No

Other facilities: Audio guide (in Romanian, English, French, and German), Toilets, Gift shop

**Get back to Brașov from Sinaia:**

*By bus:* for schedules and rates, see http://www.autogari.ro

*By train:* for schedules and rates, see http://www.infofer.ro/en/

*By car:* Take E60 (to Brașov) via Bușteni, Azuga, and Predeal.

Distance: 48 km; Time: 54'

# C) Râşnov, Bran & Cheile Grădiştei

Get to Râşnov:

*By bus:* for schedules and rates, see http://www.autogari.ro
*By car:* Take E574 (to Piteşti). Distance: 19 km; Time: 24'

See in Râşnov:

## Râşnov Fortress

Why go there: The road to this very well kept 14th century fortress is awe-inspiring in every season. Best tip: walk to the fortress! [The fortress can be visited via the specifically-provided bus or via the modern elevator.]
Opening hours: 9am-5pm (Mon-Sun)
Address: Râşnov
Telephone: +40734114304
Admission fee: 12 lei (adults); 6 lei (children)
Credit card accepted? No
Other facilities: Guide (in Romanian, English, and French), Restaurant, Café, Toilets, Gift shop, Parking

# Valea Cetăţii Cave

Why go there: It's the most modern show cave in Romania and the backdrop is amazing!

Opening hours: Summer (May-September): 10am-8pm & Winter (October-April): 10am-6pm

Address: 1.5 km from Râşnov Fortress

Telephone: +40268230109

Admission fee: 15 lei (adults); 10 lei (children)

Credit card accepted? No

Other facilities: Guide (in Romanian, English, and Spanish), Parking

**Get from Râşnov to Bran:**

*By bus:* for schedules and rates, see http://www.autogari.ro

*By car:* Continue on E574 (to Piteşti). Distance: 13 km; Time: 14'

**See in Bran:**

# Bran Castle

Why go there: Don't center your mind around legends; the energy of this place and its location are definitely worth a visit!

Opening hours: Summer (01.05-30.09): 12pm-6pm (Mon); 9am-6pm (Tue-Sun) & Winter (01.10-30.04): 12pm-4pm (Mon); 9am-4pm (Tue-Sun)

Address: Bran

Telephone: +40268237700

Admission fee: 35 lei (adults); 25 lei (adults aged over 65); 20 lei (students); 7 lei (primary and secondary school students)

Credit card accepted? Yes
Other facilities: Guide (in Romanian, English, and French), Audio
guide (in Romanian, English, French, and German; Price: 10 lei),
Toilets, Gift shop, 7 craftsmen stands in Bran Castle Park

**Get from Bran to Cheile Grădiştei:**

*By car:* Take E574 (to Moieciu) and continue on 112F to Cheile
Grădiştei Moieciu. Then, continue on the newly-paved road for
5 more km to Cheile Grădiştei Fundata. The view over Piatra
Craiului Mountains is amazing! Distance: 12 km; Time: 30'
*By taxi:* +40758296301, +40760595488, +40728014055 (Taxi
Bran), Uber - around 33 lei.

**Get back to Braşov from Bran:**

*By bus:* for schedules and rates, see http://www.autogari.ro
*By car:* Take E574 to Braşov (via Râşnov and Cristian). Distance:
29 km; Time: 36'

# What to pack

*In winter:* gloves/mittens, scarf, hats/ear muffins, thick clothes, lots of layers
*In summer:* sun lotion
*Year-round:* camera, raincoat, pool towel, swimsuit, flip-flops, trekking boots, smart clothes if you plan to go out in the evenings [Romanians love to dress up]

# Don't miss out on

**Romanian traditional products:** Beer, bread, cheese, fruit and vegetables, mineral water, pastry and cakes, wine

**Desserts:**

Gomboți – Plum dumplings
Kürtös Kalács – Chimney cake [buy them fresh from the main roads while driving around Transylvania]
Papanași – Dumplings with sour cream and jam
Somlói galuska – Sponge cake with vanilla sauce, chocolate, rum, walnuts, and whipped cream

**Events:**

Seven weeks before Easter – Pancake Caravan/Fasching: In Prejmer, there is a festival/carnival dating back to ancient times; according to the legend, the noise and the cheerfulness of the locals was meant to drive away the bad spirits.

**Get to Prejmer:**

*By bus:* for schedules and rates, see http://www.autogari.ro
*By train:* for schedules and rates, see http://www.infofer.ro/en/
*By car:* Take E574 (to Sf. Gheorghe) and turn right at the first
crossroads after exiting Härman. Distance: 22 km; Time: 28'

**See in Prejmer:**

# Prejmer Fortified Church

Why go there: UNESCO World Heritage Site, the only
fortress/fortified church in the region that could not be taken
by the Turks mainly due to the robustness and thickness of the
walls.
Opening hours: Summer (01.05-30.09): 9am-5pm (Tue-Fri);
9am-3pm (Sat); 11am-5pm (Sun); Mon: closed & Winter (01.10-
30.04): 9am-3pm (Tue-Sat); Sun-Mon: closed
Address: Prejmer
Telephone: +40268362052
Admission fee: 8 lei (adults); 4 lei (students)
Credit cards accepted? No
Facilities: Toilets (only in summer)

## Get back to Braşov:

*By bus:* for schedules and rates, see http://www.autogari.ro

*By train:* for schedules and rates, see http://www.infofer.ro/en/

By car: Take E574 (to Braşov) via Hărman. Distance: 17 km;
Time: 20'

# Things You Need to Know

## Getting into the city

### If arriving by plane:

The main hub is Henri Coandă (Otopeni) Airport in Bucharest. Get from the airport to Bucharest center and/or continue to Braşov:

*By bus:* for schedules and rates, see http://mementobus.com/; *for best rates, book in advance.* Also check http://www.cdyservice.ro/ (only in Romanian, ask for help).

*By train:* Henri Coandă Express to Gara de Nord (via shuttle bus) (5:45am-9:12pm). One-way ticket: 6.80 lei
Trains run to Braşov from Gara de Nord; for schedules and rates, see http://www.infofer.ro/en/

*By taxi:* You shouldn't pay more than 40 lei to get from Otopeni Airport to Gara de Nord.

### If arriving by train:

There are international trains from Budapest and Vienna arriving in summer and in winter to Braşov railway station. Get from the railway station to Braşov center:

*By bus:* Take Bus no. 4 to Livada Poştei. Ticket: 2 lei

*By taxi:* You should pay around 10 lei for a ride from the railway station to the center.

## If arriving by bus:

Autogara Vest (Şos. Cristianului) provides connections to Austria, Czech Republic, Denmark, France, Germany, Hungary, Italy, Moldova, Norway, Slovenia, Sweden, Switzerland, The Netherlands, etc. Get from the bus station to Braşov center:

*By bus:* Take Bus no. 16 to Livada Poştei. Ticket: 2 lei

*By taxi:* You should pay around 8 lei for a ride from the bus station to the center.

## If arriving by car:

Rent a car at the airport or search for better deals online and pick the car up in Bucharest or Braşov. The recommended route to Braşov is E60: Ploieşti – Sinaia – Buşteni – Azuga – Predeal – Braşov.

*You can park your car in Braşov (Mon-Sat, 8am-8pm) even if you don't have local coins, by sending the following text to 7420:*

*- 341 REGISTRATION PLATE [Cost: EUR 0.4 + VAT(24%)/hour]*

*- 342 REGISTRATION PLATE [Cost: EUR 2.6 + VAT(24%)/day]*

# Transportation tips

**By bus:**
Regular ticket price: 2 lei
Ticket to Poiana Braşov: 5 lei
1-day pass: 10 lei
10 rides: 20 lei

Don't forget to validate your ticket/electronic pass when you get on the bus. Have an ID card on you if you opt for passes.

*You can buy tickets and passes from big bus stops (search for a 'RAT' sign) and sometimes from kiosks and small shops near the stops. There are also ticket vending machines at some of the stops. Have cash and coins on you.*

*As of 01.07.2015, your bus ticket is valid for 50 minutes on several bus numbers. Consequently, change buses at will until you run out of time.*

**By taxi:**
A.T.I.: +40268417777
Martax: +40268313040
RO: +40268319999
Tod: +40268321111

Approved rate/km: 1.73 lei (during the day); 1.93 lei (during the night: 10pm-6am)

Always look at the rate listed on the door of the taxi and check to see if the meter is running!

*Download the free 'Clever Taxi' app on your smartphone; locate your position and order. Specify if you wish to pay by credit card or by cash.*

*As of November 2016, we also have Uber in Braşov. Got your app? Use it! [For rides to Poiana Braşov, there is a fixed rate: 40 lei (regular car), 50 lei (car with sports equipment rack)].*

# Money – ATMs, credit cards & the currency

The Romanian currency is the *leu*. It is subdivided into 100 *bani* and its name means 'lion'.

Dollars and Euros can easily be exchanged at currency exchange bureaus [please check commission!] and in banks.

ATMs are frequent in towns and you will find many stores, hotels/guesthouses/hostels, and restaurants/pubs/bars/cafés/clubs that accept payments by credit card. It is however advisable to always have a decent amount of money on you, as it is difficult to find ATMs/use credit cards in remote villages.

# Useful local phrases

Romanian is part of the great family of Indo-European languages, the Romance language branch, the Eastern Romance language sub branch and Italian is the Romance language that Romanian resembles most. The distinction between formal and informal resides in the fact that people closer to the addressor's status and age tend to be addressed in the 2nd person singular while people of higher status or age tend to be addressed in the 2nd person plural.

You will not have a hard time finding English speakers in Braşov and in all the other Romanian cities, as almost all youngsters are studying English at school. If you find yourselves in the rural areas of the country, people will tend to speak German, Hungarian, or sometimes French, so the following phrases might come in handy:

Thank you. – Mulţumesc. [mool-tzu-MESK]
You're welcome. – Cu plăcere. [koo pluh-CHAIR-eh]
Please – Te rog *(informal)* [teh ROHG] / Vă rog *(formal)* [vuh ROHG]
Yes – Da [DAH]
No – Nu [NOO]
Hello. – Bună. *(informal)* [BOO-nuh]
Good morning. – Bună dimineaţa. [BOO-nuh dee-mee-NYAH-tzuh]
Good afternoon. – Bună ziua. [BOO-nuh zee-wah]
Good evening. – Bună seara. [BOO-nuh syah-ruh]
Good night. – Noapte bună. [NWAHP-teh BOO-nuh]
Goodbye. – Pa *(informal)* [PAH] / La revedere *(formal)* [lah reh-veh-DEH-reh]
What's your name? – Cum te cheamă? *(informal)* [coom teh

KYAHM-uh] / Cum vă cheamă? *(formal)* [coom vuh KYAHM-uh]

My name is... – Mă numesc... [MUH noo- MESK...]

How are you? – Ce faci? *(informal)* [cheh FAHTCH] / Ce faceți? *(formal)* [cheh FAHTCHEHTZI]

I'm fine. – Sunt bine. [SOONT BEE-neh]

How much does it cost? – Cât costă? [COOHT KOHS-tah]

How can I get to...? – Cum ajung la...? [COOM ah-ZHOONG lah]

I don't understand. – Nu înțeleg. [NOO oohn-tzeh-LEG]

Help! – Ajutor! [ah-zhoo-TOR]

Bus ticket – Bilet de autobuz [BEEH-let deh A-OO-toh-booz]

1-day pass – Abonament de o zi [a-BOH-na-ment deh o ZEE]

Train ticket – Bilet de tren [BEEH-let deh TREN]

# Accommodation

**4 Cardinal's**
Area: Business Center
Address: Strada Gheorghe Lazăr nr. 19
Telephone: +40723221897
Price range: $$$$ (40-60)
Credit card accepted? No

**Alpin Hotel**
Telephone: +40268262343
Area: Poiana Braşov
Price range: $$$$$ (60-80)
Credit card accepted? Yes
Website: http://www.hotelalpin.ro/en/

**Cubix Hotel**
Area: Astra District, close to the commercial area of Braşov
Address: Bulevardul Saturn nr. 47
Telephone: +40368006010
Price range: $$$$$ (60-80)
Credit card accepted? Yes
Website: http://www.hotelcubix.ro/

**Drachenhaus Hotel**
Area: Old Town
Address: Strada Nicolae Bălcescu nr. 12
Telephone: +40368401606
Price range: $$$$ (40-60)
Credit card accepted? Yes
Website: http://www.drachenhaus.ro/en/

## Ecaterina

Area: Downtown
Address: Strada Ecaterina Varga nr. 15, ap. 3
Telephone: +40744329423
Price range: $$ (10-20)
Credit card accepted? No, but you can pay by credit card when you book online

## Writers' Residence

Area: Downtown
Address: Strada Crişan nr. 18
Telephone: +40744329423
Price range: $$ (10-20)
Credit card accepted? No, but you can pay by credit card when you book online

## Rolling Stone Hostel

Area: Schei District, close to Old Town
Address: Strada Piatra Mare 2A
Telephone: +40268513965
Price range: $$ (10-20)
Credit card accepted? No
Website: http://www.rollingstone.ro/

# Restaurants

**Breakfast:**

**La Plăcinte**
Moldovan Restaurant
Opening hours: 10am – 11pm (Mon-Sun)
Address: Bd. Gării nr. 7
Telephone: +40743110053
Price range: $ (5-10)
Website: http://laplacinte.ro/en/
Credit card accepted? Yes
Recommendations: Moldovan pies - sweet or salty -, traditional dishes, and exquisite desserts and drinks. What can I say? The menu is fascinating! P.S. They have breakfast specials. Ask!

**Zoomserie**
Dessert Restaurant
Opening hours: 8am – 10pm (Mon-Sun)
Address: Strada Apollonia Hirscher nr. 1
Telephone: +40743023023
Price range: $$ (10-20)
Credit card accepted? Yes
Website: http://www.zoomserie.ro/
Recommendations: You will spend your first 5 to 10 minutes staring at the cakes. Only after, will you be ready to place your order. I don't know why, but the Banoffee Pie won me over.

## Lunch:

**Bistro de l'Arte**
(mainly) French Restaurant
Opening hours: 9am – 1am (Mon-Sat); 12pm-1am (Sun)
Address: Piața George Enescu nr. 11bis
Telephone: +40720535566
Price range: $$ (10-20)
Credit card accepted? Yes
Website: http://www.bistrodelarte.ro/
Recommendations: The menu is ever-changing, while old favourites are brought back into the spotlight! The soups are delicious, so are the vegetarian dishes and the desserts!

**Maestro**
Romanian Restaurant
Opening hours: 9am – 11pm (Mon-Sun)
Address: Strada Avram Iancu nr. 52
Telephone: +40268415958
Price range: $ (5-10)
Credit card accepted? Yes
Website: http://www.maestro-restaurant.ro/
Recommendations: The dishes are very tasty and good value. The papanași served here are delicious and amongst the best in town!

## Dinner:

**Amasi**
Lebanese Restaurant
Opening hours: 9am – 11:30pm (Mon-Sat); 11am – 11pm (Sun)
Address: Strada Mihai Viteazul nr. 1
Telephone: +40368454033
Price range: $$ (10-20)

Credit card accepted? Yes
Website: http://www.amasi.ro/
Recommendations: The savory Fatus and the delicious Kashta for dessert.

**Millenium**
International Restaurant
Opening hours: 10am – 12am (Mon-Sun)
Address: Strada Negoiu nr. 14
Telephone: +40268412363
Price range: $$ (10-20)
Credit card accepted? Yes
Website: http://www.bistro-millenium.ro/
Recommendations: Ratatouille, the apple cake, Romanian specialties.

**Passage**
Burger Restaurant
Opening hours: 09:30am – 11pm (Mon-Sun)
Address: Strada Carpenului nr. 1A
Telephone: +40755077833
Price range: $$ (10-20)
Credit card accepted? Yes
Website: https://www.facebook.com/passagebar/
Recommendations: Veggie burger, parmesan & garlic fries.

# Nightlife

**Have fun:**

**Arta**
Pool & games
Opening hours: 16pm – 12am (Mon-Thu; Sun); 12pm – 1am (Fri-Sat)
Address: Strada Grădinarilor nr. 13
Telephone: +40722566564
Price range: $ (5-10)
Credit card accepted? Yes
Website: http://www.clubarta.ro/
Recommendations: Have a fun night out and enjoy a nice game of pool, darts, poker, or ping-pong.

**Cinema One**
Cinema
Address: Coresi Shopping Resort, Strada Zaharia Stancu nr. 1
Telephone: +0737759658
Price range: $ (5-10)
Credit card accepted? Yes
Website: http://www.cinemaone.ro/en/
Recommendations: Book your ticket online and arrive to claim it 30 minutes before the movie starts playing.

**Opt for relaxation:**

**Opera Braşov**
Opera House
Address: Strada Bisericii Române nr. 51
Telephone: +40268415990
Price range: $ (5-10)
Credit card accepted? No

Website: http://www.opera-brasov.ro/
Recommendations: There are great opera and ballet shows here, but be sure to buy tickets ahead, because they tend to sell out very fast.

**Rope Street Museum**
Museum & Café
Address: Strada Cerbului nr. 13
Telephone: +40731909999
Price range: $ (5-10)
Credit card accepted? Yes
Website: https://www.facebook.com/RopeStreetBrasov/
Recommendations: Smiles, photographs, legends, free maps, good tea and cakes. P.S. If you stop for snacks, you don't need to pay for the visit to the museum itself. It's included.

**Go out for a drink:**

**Ceainăria Open Heart**
Teahouse
Opening hours: 9am – 12am (Mon-Sun)
Address: Strada Michael Weiss nr. 18
Telephone: +40756112289
Price range: $ (5-10)
Credit card accepted? Yes
Website: http://www.openheart.ro/
Recommendations: The smoothies and milkshakes are great and be sure to ask for a bowl of cookies to savor. Braşov's Old Town will feel closest. How about a mate savored in the crisp air creeping in through the enormous windows?

## Galleria Art and Coffee

Café

Opening hours: 08am – 12am (Mon-Fri); 09am – 12am (Sat); 09:30am – 12:30am (Sun)

Address: Strada Colonel Buzuioanu nr. 1

Telephone: +40742800100

Price range: $ (5-10)

Credit card accepted? Yes

Recommendations: Cookie - the Oreo smoothie that will drive you crazy, plus the many delightful lemonades served.

## Lavender Cake & Wine Bar

Cake & Wine Bar

Opening hours: 09am – 09pm (Mon-Sun)

Address: Strada Calcarului nr. 19B

Telephone: +40743885788

Price range: $$ (10-20)

Credit card accepted? Yes

Website: https://www.facebook.com/lavendercafebrasov/

Recommendations: Cakes and drinks alike. Exquisite.

## Tucano Coffee

Coffee shop

Opening hours: 10am – 10pm (Mon-Sun)

Address: Strada Zaharia Stancu nr. 1

Telephone: +40773748350

Price range: $$ (10-20)

Credit card accepted? Yes

Website: http://www.tucanocoffee.com/

Recommendations: Best cheesecakes in town. Colours, handmade items, you'll drool and drool and drool.

**Go dancing:**

**The Vintage Pub**
Opening hours: 12pm – 5am (Mon-Sun)
Address: Strada Livada Poştei nr. 1
Telephone: +40745050487
Price range: $$ (10-20)
Credit card accepted? Yes
Website: http://www.thevintagepub.ro/
Recommendations: This is a club and a pub at the same time.
There are parties Thursday to Saturday, so be sure to check
their updates on Facebook if you want to join the celebrations.

# Holidays and Traditions

March 1st – Mărţişor: The first day of spring; men give women
small objects bound with a red and white string for luck and
health during the following year.
March 8th – International Women's Day: Much celebrated in
Romania; men give flowers to their mothers, wives, girlfriends,
and women friends on this day.
First Sunday after Easter – Junii: The men from Schei ride into
town to celebrate the crossover from winter to spring.
May 20th (or around this date) – The Long Night of Museums
December 6th (or around this date) – The lighting up of the
Christmas tree in Council Square

Easter Eve: Join a Romanian family and paint the Easter eggs.
December 5th: Join a Romanian family for St. Nicholas Eve and
exchange small but meaningful gifts.
December – February: Rediscover the child in you and build a
snowman by yourself or with the help of friends.

# Sports

## Ice-skating

Patinoarul Olimpia; Strada Coşbuc nr. 2; +40268474014
Patinoarul Olimpic *(year-round)*; Strada Turnului;
+40368442241 [Check out the Facebook page[1] of the local
hockey team for future hockey games; the atmosphere is
incredible at all these games.]
Poiana Braşov Skating Rink; Poiana Braşov (near the stadium);
+40268262355
Complex Agrement; Aleea Brediceanu Tiberiu; +40724557312

**Paragliding** - http://paramania.ro/en/
**Kiting** - http://comefly.ro/
**Skiing** - http://www.poianabrasov.com/
**Snowboarding** - http://www.poianabrasov.com/

## Trekking

Mount Tâmpa (964 m); Departure: 'Star' Department Store;
Marking: Red triangle; Time: 1.5 hrs

Mount Tâmpa (via Gabony Steps, 964 m); Departure: 'Star'
Department Store; Marking: Yellow triangle; Time: 1.5 hrs

Poiana Braşov (1020 m); Departure: Pietrele lui Solomon [reach
it by bus line 50b from Livada Poştei Bus Stop]; Marking: Red
band; Time: 1.3-2 hrs

Postăvaru Chalet (1604 m); Departure: Schei Gate; Marking:
Blue band; Time: 5 hrs

Piatra Mare Peak (1844 m); Departure: Dâmbu Morii [reach it
by bus line 17b]; Marking: Red Band; Time: 1 day (return)

---

1   https://www.facebook.com/corona.brasov.wolves

# Wildlife

Animal watching: Go animal watching in the upper part of Răcădău District around midnight. You might see foxes, brown bears, hedgehogs, sometimes even wild boar. Be careful and bear in mind that these are wild animals and their reactions are unpredictable. Do not get very close and do not try to feed them!

**Braşov Zoo**
Opening hours: 9am-6pm [Tue-Sun, in winter; Mon: closed] & 9am-8pm [Tue-Sun, in summer; Mon: closed]
Address: Strada Brazilor nr. 1
Telephone: +40268337787
Ticket: 10 lei (adults), 5 lei (children), 4 lei (groups - children), 8 lei (groups - adults)
Credit card accepted? No
Recommendations: Set in the forest, this zoo is a very special one because it combines the love for animals with a very healthy walk in the nature.

# Additional websites for information

**Braşov Map** [enter the name of the street that you are looking for] - http://www.hartabrasovului.ro/cauta-o-strada.html

**Braşov Center Map** - http://www.romaniatourism.com/romania-maps/brasov-city-map-harta-orasului.html

**Local Bus Map & Timetable** - http://www.ratbv.ro/routes-and-timetables/

**Online Railway Tickets | CFR** - https://bilete.cfrcalatori.ro/

**Online Railway Tickets | Regio** - https://regiotrans.blueticket.ro/ (only in Romanian)

**Online Railway Tickets | Softrans** - http://rezervari.softrans.ro/ (only in Romanian)

**Translators & Interpreters** - http://www.traduci.biz/

# Useful phone numbers

112 Emergency Call (Police, Firemen, Medical Emergencies)
+40268952 Railway information
+40268320022 Braşov Emergency Hospital
+40268332143; +40268421848 Nonstop pharmacies
+40268407500 Braşov Police Department
+40268428888 Braşov Fire Department
+40268413951 Bureau of Consumer Protection
+40268471260 Main Post Office

# Random tips

Romanian Holidays – check for the opening times of the attractions and of the restaurants/pubs/bars/cafés/clubs before going:

January 1st – New Year
January 2nd – New Year
April/May – Orthodox Easter (Easter Sunday & Easter Monday)
May 1st – Labor Day
May/June – Pentecost (Pentecost Sunday & Pentecost Monday)
August 15th – St. Mary
November 30th – St. Andrew
December 1st – Romanian National Day
December 25th – Christmas Day
December 26th – Boxing Day

Almost all restaurants/pubs/bars/cafés/clubs and hotels/guesthouses/hostels offer free Wi-Fi. Just ask for the password!

Tips are recommended in restaurants/pubs/bars/cafés/clubs and usually amount to 10% of your check.

There are several grocery stores open 24 hours: Bulevardul Victoriei nr. 3 (Profi), Strada Saturn nr. 1 (Profi), Strada Griviței nr. 38 (Sergiana).

Tickets for bus rides to villages and towns outside Brașov should be bought from the bus drivers.

Train tickets specified are for 2nd class.

The prices and details specified are those valid on December 1st 2016.

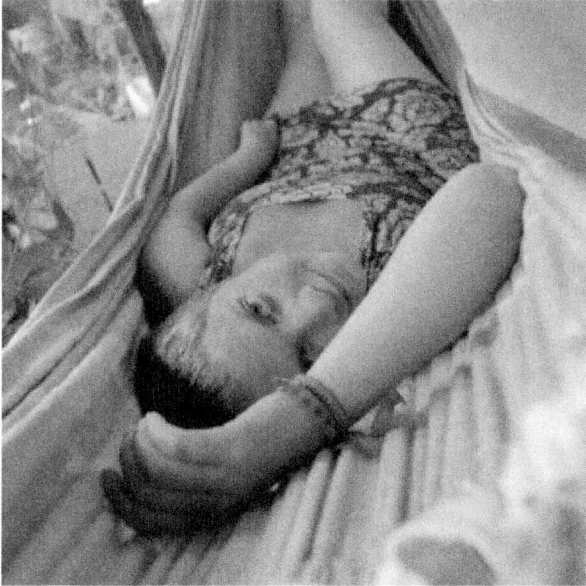

# About the Author

## Olivia-Petra Coman

I'm an adventurous, extravagant, and vegetarian traveler, crazy about extreme water sports.

I travel the world to discover its hidden treasures, I dream to get to the historical sites that I've only explored in books, and I hope to make a difference through my work and vision of the world around me.

Travel writing has always been on my mind, because traveling is no longer a passion, but a part of me. There are so many more off-the-beaten-track destinations and I can't wait to discover them and to live to tell/write about them!

Twitter: @oliviapetra

Blog: http://blog.inreperta.com

Photography © Marcel Băncilă | marcelbancila@gmail.com

# Unanchor
## Chief Itinerary Coordinator

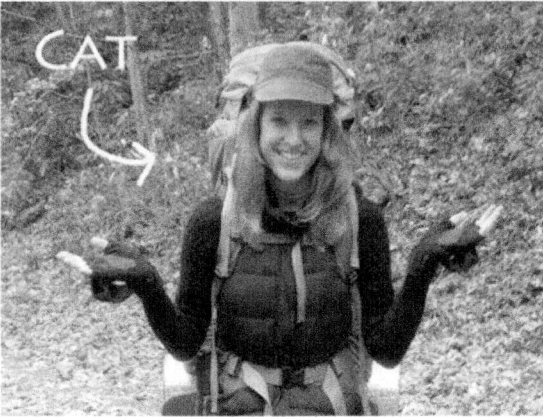

# Unanchor wants your opinion!

Your next travel adventure starts now. A simple review on Amazon will grant you and a travel buddy, friend, or human of your choosing any of the wonderful Unanchor digital itineraries for free.

**What a deal!**

**Leave a Review**

- Leave a review: http://www.amazon.com/unanchor

**Collect your guides**

- Send an email to reviews@unanchor.com with a link to your review.
- Wait with bated breath.
- Receive your new travel adventure in your inbox!

# Get Inspired! Other Unanchor Itineraries

## Africa

One Day in Africa - A Guide to Tangier
Cape Town - What not to miss on a 4-day first-timers' itinerary
Johannesburg/Pretoria: A 4-Day South Africa Tour Itinerary
Africa

## Asia

4 Days in Bishkek On a Budget
Beijing Must Sees, Must Dos, Must Eats - 3-Day Tour Itinerary
2 Days in Shanghai: A Budget-Conscious Peek at Modern China
A 3-Day Tryst with 300-Year-Old Kolkata
Kolkata (Calcutta): 2 Days of Highlights
3-Day Budget Delhi Itinerary
Delhi in 3 Days - A Journey Through Time
3 Days Highlights of Mumbai
Nozawa Onsen's Winter Secrets - A 3-Day Tour
3-Day Highlights of Tokyo
Tour Narita During an Airport Layover
3 Days in the Vibrant City of Seoul and the Serene Countryside of Gapyeong
A First Timer's Weekend Guide to Ulaanbaatar
The Very Best of Moscow in 3 Days
Saint Petersburg in Three Days

## Central America and the Caribbean

Old San Juan, Puerto Rico 2-Day Walking Itinerary
Two Exciting Days in Dutch Sint Maarten - Hello Cruisers!
Two Amazing Days in St. Croix, USVI - Hello Cruisers!

# Europe

Beginner's Iceland - A four-day self-drive itinerary
Mostar - A City with Soul in 1 Day
3 Days in Brussels - The grand sites via the path less trodden
Zagreb For Art Lovers: A Three-Day Itinerary
3-Day Prague Beer Pilgrimage
Best of Prague - 3-Day Itinerary
3 Days in Copenhagen - Explore Like a Local
Best of Copenhagen 2-Day Walking Itinerary
Christmas in Copenhagen - A 2-Day Guide
3 Days in Helsinki
Highlights of Budapest in 3 Days
3 Days in Dublin City - City Highlights, While Eating & Drinking Like a Local
Weekend Break: Tbilisi - Crown Jewel of the Caucasus
2 Days In Berlin On A Budget
A 3-Day Guide to Berlin, Germany
3 Days of Fresh Air in Moldova's Countryside
Amsterdam 3-Day Alternative Tour: Not just the Red Light District
Amsterdam Made Easy: A 3-Day Guide
Two-day tour of Utrecht: the smaller, less touristy Amsterdam!
Krakow: Three-Day Tour of Poland's Cultural Capital
Best of Warsaw 2-Day Itinerary
Lisbon in 3 Days: Budget Itinerary
Braşov - Feel the Pulse of Transylvania in 3 Days
Lausanne 1-Day Tour Itinerary
Belgrade: 7 Days of History on Foot

# France

Paris to Chartres Cathedral: 1-Day Tour Itinerary
A 3-Day Tour of Mont St Michel, Normandy and Brittany
Art Lovers' Paris: A 2-Day Artistic Tour of the City of Lights
Paris 1-Day Itinerary - Streets of Montmartre
Paris 3-Day Walking Tour: See Paris Like a Local
Paris 4-Day Winter Wonderland
Paris for Free: 3 Days
The Best of Paris in One Day

# Greece

Athens 3-Day Highlights Tour Itinerary
Chania & Sfakia, Greece & Great Day Trips Nearby (5-Day Itinerary)
Santorini, Greece in 3 Days: Living like a Local
2-Day Beach Tour: Travel like a Local in Sithonia Peninsula, Halkidiki, Greece
Day Trip From Thessaloniki to Kassandra Peninsula, Halkidiki, Greece
Thessaloniki, Greece - 3-Day Highlights Itinerary

# Italy

A Day on Lake Como, Italy
3-Day Florence Walking Tours
Florence, Italy 3-Day Art & Culture Itinerary
Milan Unknown - A 3-day tour itinerary
3 Days of Roman Adventure: spending time and money efficiently in Rome
A 3-Day Tour Around Ancient Rome
Discover Rome's Layers: A 3-Day Walking Tour
See Siena in a Day
Landscape, Food, & Trulli: 1 Week in Puglia, the Valle d'Itria, and Matera
Three Romantic Walks in Venice

# Spain

3-Day Highlights of Barcelona Itinerary
FC Barcelona: More than a Club (A 1-Day Experience)
Ibiza on a Budget - Three-Day Itinerary
Three days exploring Logroño and La Rioja by public transport
Málaga, Spain – 2-Day Tour from the Moors to Picasso
Mijas - One Day Tour of an Andalucían White Village
Two-Day Tour in Sunny Seville, Spain
Best of Valencia 2-Day Guide

# United Kingdom

Bath: An Exploring Guide - 2-Day Itinerary
History, Culture, and Craic: 3 Days in Belfast, Ireland
2-Day Brighton Best-of Walks & Activities
Bristol in 2 Days: A Local's Guide
Two-Day Self-Guided Walks - Cardiff
The Best of Edinburgh: A 3-Day Journey from Tourist to Local

*3-Day London Tour for Olympic Visitors*
*An Insider's Guide to the Best of London in 3 Days*
*Done London? A 3-day itinerary for off the beaten track North Norfolk*
*London 1-Day Literary Highlights*
*London for Free :: Three-Day Tour*
*London's Historic City Wall Walk (1-2 days)*
*London's South Bank - Off the Beaten Track 1-Day Tour*
*London's Villages - A 3-day itinerary exploring Hampstead, Marylebone and Notting Hill*
*Low-Cost, Luxury London - 3-Day Itinerary*
*The 007 James Bond Day Tour of London*
*MADchester - A Local's 3-Day Guide To Manchester*
*One Day in Margate, UK on a Budget*

# Middle East

*Paphos 3-Day Itinerary: Live like a local!*
*Adventure Around Amman: A 2-Day Itinerary*
*Amman 2-Day Cultural Tour*
*Doha 2-Day Stopover Cultural Tour*
*Doha Surf and Turf: A two-day itinerary*
*3 Days as an Istanbulite: An Istanbul Itinerary*
*Between the East and the West, a 3-Day Istanbul Itinerary*

# North America

## Canada

*Relax in Halifax for Two Days Like a Local*
*An Insider's Guide to Toronto: Explore the City Less Traveled in Three Days*
*The Best of Toronto - 2-Day Itinerary*
*Toronto: A Multicultural Retreat (3-day itinerary)*

# Mexico

Cancun and Mayan Riviera 5-Day Itinerary (3rd Edition)
Everything to see or do in Mexico City - 7-Day Itinerary
Mexico City 3-Day Highlights Itinerary
Todo lo que hay que ver o hacer en la Ciudad de México  - Itinerario de 7 Dias
Your Chiapas Adventure: San Cristobal de las Casas and Palenque, Mexico 5-Day
Itinerary

# United States

## East Coast

Girls' 3-Day Weekend Summer Getaway in Asheville, NC
Atlanta 3-Day Highlights
Baltimore: A Harbor, Parks, History, Seafood & Art - 3-Day Itinerary
Boston 2-Day Historic Highlights Itinerary
Navigating Centuries of Boston's Nautical History in One Day
Rainy Day Boston One-Day Itinerary
Brooklyn, NY 2-Day Foodie Tour
The Weekenders Guide To Burlington, Vermont
A Local's Guide to the Hamptons 3 Day Itinerary
Weekend Day Trip from New York City: The Wine & Whiskey Trail
2 Days Exploring Haunted Key West
3 Day PA Dutch Country Highlights (Lancaster County, PA)
Day Trek Along the Hudson River
A Local's Guide to Montauk, New York in 2 Days - From the Ocean to the Hills
New Haven Highlights: Art, Culture & History 3-Day Itinerary
Day Trip from New York City: Mountains, Falls, & a Funky Town
3-Day Amazing Asian Food Tour of New York City!
Hidden Bars of New York City's East Village & Lower East Side: A 2-Evening
Itinerary
Jewish New York in Two Days
Lower Key, Lower Cost: Lower Manhattan - 1-Day Itinerary
New York City - First Timer's 2-Day Walking Tour
New York City's Lower East Side, 1-Day Tour Itinerary
New York Like A Native: Five Boroughs in Six Days
3-Day Discover Orlando Itinerary
Five Days in the Wild Outer Banks of North Carolina
Two Days in Philadelphia

*Pittsburgh: Three Days Off the Beaten Path*
*Day Trip from New York City: Heights of the Hudson Valley (Bridges and Ridges)*
*RVA Haunts, History, and Hospitality: Three Days in Richmond, Virginia*
*Savannah 3-Day Highlights Itinerary*
*Three Days in the Sunshine City of St. Petersburg, Florida*
*Washington, DC in 4 Days*
*Washington, DC: 3 Days Like a Local*

## Central US

*A Laid-Back Long Weekend in Austin, TX*
*3-Day Chicago Highlights Itinerary*
*6-Hour "Layover" Chicago*
*Chicago Food, Art and Funky Neighborhoods in 3 Days*
*Famous Art & Outstanding Restaurants in Chicago 1-Day Itinerary*
*Family Weekend in Columbus, OH*
*Ohio State Game Day Weekend*
*Corpus Christi: The Insider Guide for a 4-Day Tour*
*The Best of Kansas City: 3-Day Itinerary*
*La Grange, Kentucky: A 3-Day Tour Itinerary*
*Louisville: Three Days in Derby City*
*New Orleans 3-Day Itinerary*
*Paris Foodie Classics: 1 Day of French Food*
*Wichita From Cowtown to Air Capital in 2 Days*

## West Coast

*Orange County 3-Day Budget Itinerary*
*Cruisin' Asbury like a Local in 1 Day*
*A Day on Bainbridge Island*
*Beverly Hills, Los Angeles - 1-Day Tour*
*Beer Lovers 3-Day Guide To Northern California*
*The Best of Boulder, CO: A Three-Day Guide*
*Lesser-known Oahu in 4 Days on a Budget*
*Local's Guide to Oahu - 3-Day Tour Itinerary*
*Summer in Jackson Hole: Local Tips for the Perfect Three to Five Day Adventure*
*Tackling 10 Must-Dos on the Big Island in 3 Days*
*Las Vegas - Gaming Destination Diversions - Ultimate 3-Day Itinerary*
*Las Vegas on a Budget - 3-Day Itinerary*
*2-Day Los Angeles Vegan and Vegetarian Foodie Itinerary*
*Downtown Los Angeles 1-Day Walking Tour*

Hollywood, Los Angeles - 1-Day Walking Tour
Los Angeles 4-Day Itinerary (partly using Red Tour Bus)
Los Angeles Highlights 3-Day Itinerary
Los Angeles On A Budget - 4-Day Tour Itinerary
Sunset Strip, Los Angeles - 1-Day Walking Tour
An Active 2-3 Days In Moab, Utah
Beyond the Vine: 2-Day Napa Tour
Wine, Food, and Fun: 3 Days in Napa Valley
Palm Springs, Joshua Tree & Salton Sea: A 3-Day Itinerary
Portland Bike and Bite: A 2-Day Itinerary
Three Days Livin' as a True and Local Portlander
Weekend Tour of Portland's Craft Breweries, Wineries, & Distilleries
Best of the Best: Three-Day San Diego Itinerary
San Francisco 2-Day Highlights Itinerary
San Francisco Foodie Weekend Itinerary
The Tech Lover's 48-Hour Travel Guide to Silicon Valley & San Francisco
Alaska Starts Here - 3 Days in Seward
Three Days in Central California's Wine Country
Tucson: 3 Days at the Intersection of Mexico, Native America & the Old West

# Oceania

The Blue Mountains: A weekend of nature, culture and history.
A Weekend Snapshot of Melbourne
An Afternoon & Evening in Melbourne's Best Hidden Bars
Laneway Melbourne: A One-Day Walking Tour
Magic of Melbourne 3-Day Tour
Two Wheels and Pair of Cozzies: the Best of Newcastle in 3 Days
Best of Perth's Most Beautiful Sights in 3 Days
A Weekend Snapshot of Sydney
Sydney, Australia - 3-Day **Best Of** Itinerary
Enjoy the Rebuild - Christchurch 2-Day Tour
The Best of Wellington: 3-Day Itinerary

# South America

An Insider's Guide to the Best of Buenos Aires in 3 Days
Buenos Aires Best Kept Secrets: 2-Day Itinerary
Sights & Sounds of São Paulo - 3-Day Itinerary
Cuenca, Ecuador - A 3-Day Discovery Tour
A 1-Day Foodie's Dream Tour of Arequipa
Arequipa - A 2-Day Itinerary for First-Time Visitors
Cusco and the Sacred Valley - a five-day itinerary for a first-time visitor
Little Known Lima 3-Day Tour

# Southeast Asia

Between the Skyscrapers - Hong Kong 3-Day Discovery Tour
Art and Culture in Ubud, Bali – 1-Day Highlights
Go with the Sun to Borobudur & Prambanan in 1 Day
A 3-Day Thrilla in Manila then Flee to the Sea
Manila on a Budget: 2-Day Itinerary
A First Timer's Guide to 3 Days in the City that Barely Sleeps - Singapore
Family Friendly Singapore - 3 Days in the Lion City
Singapore: 3 Fun-Filled Days on this Tiny Island
The Affordable Side of Singapore: A 4-Day Itinerary
The Two Worlds of Kaohsiung in 5 Days
72 Hours in Taipei: The All-rounder
Girls' Weekend in Bangkok: Shop, Spa, Savour, Swoon
The Ins and Outs of Bangkok: A 3-Day Guide
Saigon 3-Day Beyond the Guidebook Itinerary

*Unanchor is a global family for travellers to experience the world with the heart of a local.*

**UNANCHOR**

Printed in Great Britain
by Amazon